Reclaiming Food

Reclaiming Food

Emma Kathryn

This work CC-BY-NC-SA 2021 Emma Kathryn

All reproductions must be for non-commercial use only, must bear attribution to the author, and must carry this same license.

ISBN: 978-1-7357944-8-8

Ritona
an imprint of RITONA a.s.b.l
3 Rue de Wormeldange
Rodenbourg, Luxembourg
L-6995

Layout and Design: Rhyd Wildermuth
View our catalogue and online journal at
ABEAUTIFULRESISTANCE.ORG

Contents

Introduction–9

Stocks, Soups & Sauces
Meat Stock–12
Fish Stock–13
Vegetable Stock–14
Onion Stock–15
Chicken or Turkey Broth–16
Vegetable Soup–17
Roast Vegetable Soup–18
Basic White Sauce–19
Basic Gravy–20
Basic Tomato Sauce–21

Bread, Dumplings, Pastry & Fritters–23
Basic White Bread–24
Soda Bread–16
Garlic & Herb Tear n Share–27
Easy Flatbread–29
Dumplings–30
Jamaican Fried Dumplings–31
Sweetcorn Fritters–33
Basic Shortcrust Pastry–34

Comfort Food–35
Cheese & Potato Pie–36
Shepherds Pie–37
Vegetable Cottage Pie–38
Beef Casserole–39

Vegetable Stew–40
Leftover Pie–41
Pasta Bake–42
Toad in the Hole–43
Vegetable Crumble–44

Easy Meals–46
Sausage casserole–47
Corned Beef Hash–48
Savoury Breed and Butter Pudding–49
Cheese and Onion Quiche–50
Omelet–51
Spaghetti Bolognese–52
Spicy Couscous–53
Roast Vegetables with a Baked Egg–54
Easy Chicken & Rice–55
Easy Vegetable Curry–57
Pasta, Peas & Bacon with a Cheese Sauce–58

Snacks & Fillers–59
Veggie Peel Crisps–60
Bubble & Squeak–61
Baked Egg Bread & Cheese–62
Fancy Garlic Baguette–63
Sauteed Garden Peas–64
Stuffed Peppers–65
Roasted Chickpeas–66
Califlower Gratin–67
Savoury Pancakes–68
Chutney–69

Wild Eats–70

Sauteed Dandelion Stems & Leaves–71
Watercress Soup–72
Nettle Soup–73
Stewed Rabbit–74
Pan Roasted Cobnuts–76
Elderflower Fritters–77
Rosehip, Crabapple & Haw Jelly–78
Violet Honey–80
Crystallised Flowers–81
Blackberry Jam–82
Wildflower Cordial–84
Elderflower Wine–85
Blackberry & Elderberry Wine–87
Infused Spirits–88

Sweet Eats–89

Easy Custard–90
Basic Sponge–91
Ginger Cake–92
Jumble Cake–93
Banana Bread–94
Butter Biscuits–95
Frozen Fruit Yoghurt–96
Honeycomb Toffee–97
Fruit Leathers–98
Easy Rocky Road–99

Introduction

Food security is perhaps one of the biggest worries for many people, because food is one of our most basic needs. I've seen and experienced first hand how the food budget is squeezed and squashed, especially when we need to prioritise housing and the general costs involved in keeping a roof over our heads and the energy to run it.

I am passionate about food security, because I have felt the desperation that comes with not knowing where the next meal is coming from, and the constant worry about having enough to eat can be so debilitating. It felt a cookery book—focused on giving affordable, accessible recipes that are easy to make—is long overdue.

I can always remember one day, sitting at home watching a Jamie Oliver show, the premise of which was about affordable family meals. The problem with these celebrity chefs is that they are out of touch with the struggles of most workaday people. Though I can't remember the recipe he was making, he brought out a bottle of truffle oil.

That's right, *truffle oil in a show about affordable meals!*

I turned the show off straight away, as this wasn't for me or for people like me. And so you will find the recipes in this book cheap, filling, nutritious, and easy to make.

This is the second book in the *Reclaiming Ourselves* series, and while it isn't necessary that you read the first before embarking upon this one, it does provide useful information about how food security plays into the larger concept of reclaiming ourselves, of living a little more freely, of relying less on the convenience of convenience. It talks of cooking as becoming a lost skill, with many people simply unsure of how to cook simple meals from scratch using fresh produce and raw ingredients. Many people view cooking as beyond their skillset—*and yet it actually is not.*

The recipes in this book are all ones I use myself, made with ingredients that are easily accessible and do not cost "an arm and a leg." Eating well does not cost a lot of money, but you do have to forego convenience, change your shopping habits, and look at different ways of sourcing your food. But, as I have already said, the recipes here are enough to start you off on that journey and the food here is extremely accessible.

Also, keep in mind that many ideas about what is "good" are often baseless. There is nothing wrong, for example, with using frozen vegetables, and they can sometimes be more nutritious than "fresh" ones that have sat on a shop shelf for a week. When it comes to food, never be ashamed of making the most of what you have to hand.

Chapter 1
Stocks, Soups & Sauces

Stocks, sauces, and soups can form the basis of so very many meals and can enhance the plainest meal into a culinary delight. Learning how to make these from scratch is very easy and really enhances your cooking repertoire as well as making the most of the common ingredients you already have.

I often tell people if they can make a stock, they can make anything!

Meat Stock

The method for making meat stocks, at its simplest, is simply boiling the bones. This not only takes any remaining meat from the bones but also releases the marrow inside. You can use this recipe for any type of meat bone.

Ingredients

- *A pot large enough for the bones.*
- *The bones or carcass.*
- *A head of garlic depending on taste, crushed by the end of your knife or palm of your hand.*
- *2-3 sticks of celery, roughly chopped.*
- *2-3 carrots, roughly chopped.*
- *3 onions, quartered.*
- *Herbs (and here feel free to use any you have available or those you simply like the taste of though I always add a bay leaf or 2).*

Simply place all of the ingredients into your pot and fill with water so that the bones are covered. Place on the heat and bring to the boil before turning down the heat. Let it simmer for about an hour, or until the liquid has reduced by half. Then, strain into a clean container and allow to cool.

When it has cooled, you'll notice that the fat has solidified and this can be scraped off. You may also find that the stock itself has become jelly-like, and this is totally acceptable.

Fish Stock

Ingredients

- Fish bones and tails, shrimp shells, crab shell, lobster shells, etc.. Please stay clear of gills and guts when it comes to using seafood leftovers.
- 2 onions, quartered.
- 2 garlic cloves.
- 2 carrots roughly chopped.
- 2 sticks of celery, roughly chopped.
- 2 bay leaves.
- A sprig of rosemary.
- A handful of parsley.
- OPTIONAL 1 cup of white wine
- OPTIONAL 10 peppercorns.

Simply follow the same method for the meat stock and store the same way. You can use this stock in rice dishes such as risotto, or as the basis for pasta sauces to be eaten with fish. You can also use it in a white sauce (page 19) for fish pie.

Vegetable Stock

I use all of my vegetable scraps to make this, such as carrot odds and ends, onion ends, etc. I simply freeze them until needed.

Ingredients

- Vegetable scraps
- 2-3 chopped onions
- 3 carrots, roughly chopped
- At least 3 cloves of garlic (I like garlic so I use more, but you can adjust to suit your own tastes).
- 2-3 sticks of celery
- 2 sprigs of thyme
- 2 sprigs of rosemary
- 2 bay leaves

Cover with water and bring to the boil before allowing to simmer for around an hour or until the liquid has reduced by half. Strain and use straight away, refrigerate for up to three days or freeze for up to six months.

Onion Stock

This stock is easy to make and can be used as a substitute for vegetable stock.

Ingredients

- 2-3 onions quartered (keep the skins on)
- 5 cloves of garlic
- Bay leaf

Place the chopped onions in a pot with their skins. Squash the garlic cloves with the flat of a knife and add these along with enough water to fill the pot.

Place on the stove top and bring to a boil before turning down the heat and allowing the water to simmer. Cook until the water has reduced by half.

You can either use this straight away as needed, keep in the fridge for up to three days or freeze for up to six months.

Chicken or Turkey Broth

Broth is like a thin soup and is extremely nutritious. You can bulk it up by adding dumplings. The process is similar to other meat stocks.

Ingredients

- *A chicken or turkey carcass (the leftover bones and pieces)*
- *2-3 potatoes, peeled and quartered*
- *2-3 carrots, washed and chopped*
- *2 leeks, washed and chopped*

Make a meat stock with the chicken or turkey carcass (page 12) then strain, making sure you remove those little thin bones too. Add the potatoes, carrots and leeks to the liquid and return to the heat and simmer until the potatoes are soft. Serve while hot.

You can keep this in the fridge for up to three days or freeze for up to six months.

Vegetable Soup

Ingredients

- 2 onions
- 2 leeks
- 1 or 2 garlic cloves
- 2 carrots
- 1 celery stick
- Potatoes
- Vegetable stock (page 14)
- 2 tablespoons of butter
- 2 tablespoons of flour
- 300ml (11 fl oz) of water (more depending on how much liquid stock you have)

In a large pot, melt the butter over a medium heat. Chop the onion, leeks, and celery and sauté until soft, adding chopped garlic. Add the flour and mix it in before slowly adding the vegetable stock, continuously stirring until the liquid is smooth and the flour is dissolved.

Next add the rest of the vegetables and potatoes, and allow to simmer until the vegetables are cooked through and soft. Add salt, pepper, and dried herbs (for instance thyme, rosemary, or oregano) to taste.

You can make a big batch of the soup and refrigerate for up to three days or freeze for six months.

Roast Vegetable Soup

This soup is very easy to make and absolutely delicious. It is the perfect autumnal soup, but you can enjoy it anytime.

Ingredients

- *A handful of cherry tomatoes or 3 salad tomatoes*
- *Half a squash peeled and chopped*
- *2 onions, peeled and halved*
- *3 carrots, cleaned and chopped*
- *3 cloves of garlic, peeled*
- *1-2 potatoes, peeled and cubed*
- *1 green or red pepper (optional)*
- *1 litre (34 fl oz) of vegetable stock (page 14)*
- *1 tablespoon oil for roasting*

Place all of the vegetables on a baking tray (place the garlic beneath some of the other vegetables to stop it from burning) and drizzle the oil over. Place in a hot oven (350 F/ 175 C) and roast for around 20 minutes to half an hour until soft.

Remove from the oven and place the vegetables in a pot, then add the vegetable stock. For a smooth soup, I use a hand-held blender. Otherwise a potato masher will do, or you can leave the soup chunky.

Heat until hot and serve with bread for a filling meal.

Basic White Sauce

A plain white sauce to which you can then add different ingredients to create a variety of common sauces such as onion sauce, parsley and herb sauces, cheese sauces and so on.

Ingredients

- *50g (2 0z) butter*
- *50g (2 0z) flour*
- *500ml (18 fl 0z) milk*

In a medium pot or large pan, melt the butter over a medium-low (not high) heat and add the flour slowly, stirring constantly. Don't be alarmed if it forms a paste: it's supposed to.

Stir for a minute—this allows the raw flour to cook a bit. Then add the milk a little at a time, whisking constantly. You should see the lumps begin to dissolve until you have a thick velvety sauce. Take it off the heat immediately to prevent it from scorching.

This is a very basic white sauce but you can jazz it up in many ways. You can saute onions and garlic in the butter before adding the flour and milk, or you can add herbs or cheese once you have added the milk to the butter and flour.

Basic Gravy

Ingredients

- 500ml of vegetable stock (page 14)
- 1 finely chopped onion
- 1 finely chopped garlic clove
- 2 tbsp butter
- 1 tbsp flour

Melt the butter in a pan over a medium heat and just cook the onion and garlic until they are soft. Add the flour and mix it in. Don't worry if it starts to look a little like dough, this is fine. Add a little of the stock and mix in until the flour and butter is smooth and then add a little more, mixing through until you have a smooth thick liquid and add the rest of the liquid. Stir until it has thickened and serve.

For a meat gravy, follow the same process, but add meat stock and drippings (the juice and fat left over after roasting meat).

Basic Tomato Sauce

Homemade tomato sauce is delicious and easy to make, not to mention inexpensive. Jar sauces, while convenient, are full of sugar, salt, and preservatives, so much so that the leading brand in the UK carries a health warning not to consume more than once a week!

You can use this sauce for a whole range of pasta dishes and even as a pizza sauce. This recipe uses tinned (canned) tomatoes, but feel free to use fresh tomatoes, especially if you have a lot that need using up. Simply peel them using the blanching method (make a small cross in the skin and pour boiling hot water over them for 5 seconds before submerging in cold water and then the skin should just peel off) and chop them up.

Ingredients

- 1 tin of chopped tomatoes
- 2 onions, chopped
- 3 cloves of garlic, chopped
- 1 pepper, chopped (optional)
- Handful of mushrooms, sliced (optional)
- 300 ml (11fl oz) of vegetable stock
- 2 tbsp tomato puree
- 2 tbsp butter or olive oil
- A pinch of salt
- Optional: a pinch of sugar
- Dried or fresh basil or oregano

In a medium or large pot, saute the onions and garlic in butter or olive oil until soft. Add the pepper if using and cook for a minute or two more before adding the chopped tomatoes.

Mix everything together and add the stock and the tomato puree along with the mushrooms before simmering until the sauce has thickened, stirring frequently. Add the salt, sugar and dried herbs and stir through before serving.

You can easily use this as a pizza sauce, or for pasta.

You can add other ingredients to vary the sauce, for instance adding hot pepper and white wine for an spicy arrabiata. Or you can add additional vegetables or sausage for a heartier pasta sauce

Chapter 2
Bread, Dumplings, Pastry & Fritters

In this chapter you'll find recipes for bread, pastry, fritters and dumplings, all of which can help make your food go further and fill out the most basic of meals.

Basic White Bread

This recipe is easy and the bread is unlike anything you'll buy from the shops. It is thick and filling, not to mention delicious, and a little will go a long way.

A slice of this with any of the soups and broths from the previous chapter is a meal worthy of anyone!

Ingredients

- *500g (18 oz) of strong white flour (plain will do if it is all you have)*
- *1-2 tbsp salt*
- *300ml (11fl oz) of warm water*
- *2 tbsp oil*
- *1 sachet/packet of baker's yeast*

Mix the dry ingredients together in a large bowl and make a well in the middle. Combine the oil and the water in the well, then slowly mix in the dry ingredients together with the liquid until you have a dough. Don't worry if it is a little sticky.

Turn it out onto a floured surface and knead for around ten minutes. Return the dough to the bowl and cover with a damp tea towel and leave somewhere warm for the dough to proof for 45 minutes.

By this time it should have doubled in size. Turn it back out and knead again for five minutes before placing the dough in a loaf tin.

Bake in the middle of a hot oven (around 375 F/190 C) and bake for around 30 minutes until the bread is golden.

It should sound hollow when you tap it. Allow to cool before serving.

For a variation, you can add a small handful of chopped fresh rosemary or other herbs to the dough as you knead it.

If this is your first time kneading dough, it is a lot like playing with children's clay. Roll, squish, push, and then roll again, constantly returning it to a ball shape. If your hands get sticky, coat them in flour and keep going.

To clean up afterwards, take a small piece of the dough and roll it on any stuck parts and leftover flour on the surface you used. This makes cleaning much easier.

Soda Bread

This is a favourite recipe of mine. I make this whenever I want fresh bread but don't have the time to make a traditional loaf.

Ingredients

- 300g (11oz) plain flour
- 1 level teaspoon of bicarbonate of soda (baking soda)
- 250ml (9fl oz) of water

Simply sieve the dry ingredients into a mixing bowl before making a well in the centre. Add the water and mix until you have a dough. Turn out onto a lightly floured surface and knead lightly before shaping into a ball.

Place onto a baking tray and flatten slightly. Then, using a sharp knife, cut a cross into the top before placing in a hot oven and bake at around 375 F/190 C degrees until golden brown.

Garlic & Herb Tear and Share Bread

This is a simple recipe that you can make using either of the bread recipes above. This is perfect to add to a meal such as pasta.

Ingredients

- *Bread mix from either of the previous recipes*
- *150 grams of butter*
- *5 cloves of garlic, finely chopped*
- *Any herbs you have or prefer. Rosemary and thyme are my go-to herbs.*

Before you do anything else, take the butter from the fridge and leave to sit in a bowl. Make the bread dough as given in the recipes above—choose whichever you prefer.

Now mix the garlic and chopped or ground herbs in with the butter. Separate the dough into equal amounts and take a little of the butter and encase it in each piece of dough, rolling into a ball.

Place the balls onto a baking tray so that each of them are touching. Cook in the middle of a hot oven (around 375 F/ 190 C) for around 20 - 25 minutes or until golden brown. As the dough rises, the balls will merge together. Serve while they are still warm.

Easy Flatbread

This flatbread is easy and quick. You can use it to make wraps or to serve with curries, chillies, or even with pasta.

Ingredients

- *200g (8oz) flour*
- *Large pinch of salt*
- *150ml (6fl oz) water*
- *1 tbs oil*

Place the flour into a mixing bowl and add the salt. If you want, you can add herbs or spices. Make a well in the center and add the water, mixing until you have a dough that isn't too sticky. If you need to add more water, do so slowly.

Divide the dough into even portions and roll out on a floured surface until you have a rough circle shape that is around half a centimetre in thickness.

Next, add a little oil into a frying pan or skillet and place on the stove over a medium heat. Add the rolled out dough and cook for a couple of minutes on each side and serve.

Dumplings

I love dumplings in soups, stews and casseroles, especially the fluffy herby kind! Dumplings can bulk up soups and casseroles, making them more of a substantial meal, especially those that don't contain potatoes.

They are traditionally made in England using suet, a kind of fat. However, I usually use butter.

Ingredients

- 200g (8oz) self raising flour
- Large pinch of salt
- 1 tbsp of mixed herbs
- 150ml (6fl oz) water
- 1 heaped tbsp butter

Combine the dry ingredients in a bowl and add the butter, using your fingertips to mix it in.

Add the water, mixing it in until you have a sticky dough. Add more or less water or flour until you have the desired consistency. It should resemble bread mixture.

Divide the dough into equal amounts and with floured hands, form them into balls before dropping them into soups, stews and casseroles. They take about twenty minutes to cook through and should be fluffy inside.

Jamaican Fried Dumplings

Jamaican fried dumplings are one of my favourite things to make and eat and whenever I make a batch up they do not last long! They can be eaten with savoury dishes or as a sweet treat.

The best thing though is that they do not cost a lot to make and you will probably have the ingredients in your kitchen cupboard already.

Ingredients

- *3 cups of self-raising flour*
- *½ tsp salt*
- *3 tbsp butter*
- *1 cup of water*
- *Oil for frying*

Combine the flour and salt in a bowl and add the butter, using your fingertips to mix it in. Add the water slowly, stirring it in until you have a dough that isn't too sticky and turn it out onto a floured surface and knead it for a couple of minutes. Return it to the bowl and cover with a damp tea towel for around fifteen minutes.

Set a pan of oil onto a medium heat and divide the mixture into even amounts. You should get around ten dumplings from the measurements given. Roll into balls and drop into the hot oil. Fry on each side until they are a golden colour and remove from the oil.

If you wish to eat these as a savoury item, then you can serve with any kind of meal. I like to make a big batch up and serve with salsas and dips, letting people just help themselves.

They are also delicious as a sweet treat too. Simply dust them in icing or caster (powdered) sugar while they are still hot. Eat them as they are or serve with ice cream or even dip them in melted chocolate.

Sweetcorn Fritters

Fritters are a great way of using up fresh vegetables and you can make fritters using almost anything. As a child my Jamaican father would make saltfish fritters and they were my absolute favourite. Here though I am going to share with you my sweetcorn fritter recipe. I make these either as a side to larger meals or as a weekend snack. To make my sweetcorn fritters, you will need:

Ingredients

- *1 tin/can of sweetcorn, drained*
- *3 heaped tbsp of plain flour*
- *½ tsp salt*
- *1 small onion, chopped*
- *2 cloves of garlic, finely chopped*
- *½ tsp chilli flakes or powder*
- *100 ml water or 1 egg, beaten*
- *Oil for frying*

Heat the oil in a low pot or large pan over a medium heat and combine the flour, salt and chilli flakes in a large bowl and mix together before adding the rest of the ingredients. Mix them together thoroughly and drop spoonfuls of the mixture into the hot oil. Fry for around 3 minutes on each side or until they are golden brown and serve while hot.

You can substitute the sweetcorn for whatever you have, such as garden peas, chopped peppers, or onions.

Basic Shortcrust Pastry

This is my go to pastry recipe and is by far the easiest and cheapest to make. I also think it's one of the tastiest, but that's just my opinion. You can use this pastry to make pie cases, biscuits and tarts.

Ingredients

- *225g (8oz) plain flour*
- *125g (5oz) butter*
- *125g (5oz) sugar for a sweet pastry*
- *3 tbsp water or milk*

Sift the flour into a large mixing bowl (if you are wanting a sweet pastry, add the sugar now) and add the butter making sure it is cold, straight from the fridge. Use your fingertips to crumble it into the flour and add the water or milk, bringing the mixture together to form a stiff dough. Turn out onto a floured surface and roll out as needed.

You can make this in advance and keep in the fridge or even the freezer until it is needed.

Chapter 3
Comfort Food

Comfort food seems to have gotten itself something of a bad reputation over the last few years, and unjustly so if you ask me! The recipes in this section show you that comfort food can be nutritious, delicious, and substantial. They make the most of the ingredients you have and are particularly pleasing and warming on those cold and dreary days.

Cheese and Potato Pie

I'll admit, the name of this recipe is something of a misnomer because, strictly speaking, this isn't a pie. In fact there isn't any pastry at all. Instead it is a way of tarting up mashed potato, turning it into something that is very delicious and filling.

Ingredients

- *4 or 5 medium sized potatoes, quartered, boiled and mashed.*
- *100g (4oz) of cheese (or more if you want extra), grated*

Simply boil and mash your potatoes and put them in a casserole dish top with the grated cheese, spreading it evenly across the surface of the mash. Bake in a hot oven for around 10 or 15 minutes until the cheese has melted and just turned a golden colour at the edges. Serve with vegetables and gravy for a delicious easy meal.

Shepherd's Pie

This is a classic dish and always goes down well with the family whenever I make it. You will need:

Ingredients

- 4 or 5 medium sized potatoes peeled and quartered
- Milk and butter for mashing
- 400g (14oz) minced/ground beef
- 2 medium onions, chopped
- 2 garlic cloves, chopped
- 2 carrots, sliced
- 300ml (10floz) beef stock
- 100g (4oz) cheese, grated

Set the potatoes boiling and while they do, place the minced beef in a large pan with the onions and garlic and cook over a medium heat, breaking the meat up using a spatula or wooden spoon. You don't need to add any oil as the meat will cook in its own juices. Allow to cook until browned before adding the beef stock and carrots. If you wish to add any herbs, then do so now. Cook for around 10 minutes or until the stock begins to thicken

Next, drain and mash the potatoes. Place the meat in a casserole dish and top with the mashed potatoes, spreading evenly over the meat. Top the potatoes with cheese and cook in the middle of a hot oven for around twenty minutes. Serve with seasonal vegetables and gravy (page 20).

Vegetable Cottage Pie

This is a vegetarian take on the classic cottage pie and is great for vegetarians and meat eaters alike.

Ingredients

- 4 - 5 potatoes, boiled and mashed
- Half a small swede/rutabega, peeled and cubed
- 2 - 3 carrots
- Cauliflower florets
- ½ tin of garden peas or ½ cup of frozen peas
- 2 leeks
- 2 onions
- 3 cloves of garlic
- 300 ml (10fl oz) of vegetable stock
- 2 tbsp plain flour
- 2 tbsp butter
- 100g cheese (4oz)

Place the swede/rutabega, carrots, and cauliflower in a pot and bring to the boil before simmering for 5 minutes. Meanwhile, in a large pan, melt the butter and add the leeks, onions and garlic and sauté until soft. Add the flour and mix it in before adding the stock. Mix until the liquid is smooth and the flour dissolved. Add the rest of the vegetables and mix in so everything is covered in the sauce.

Transfer to an oven dish and top with the mashed potatoes before sprinkling the grated cheese on top. Bake in the middle of a hot oven for around 20 minutes and serve.

Beef Casserole

Casseroles are the perfect food for when the weather turns cooler. They are warming and filling and because of the cooking method, you can use cheaper cuts of meat, making the most of your finances and food.

This recipe is for a beef casserole but you can use this as a basis for any kind of meat casserole. There's also the added bonus of this being a complete meal and all in one pot too!

Ingredients

- 400g (14oz) stewing beef, cubed
- 3 onions, roughly chopped
- 3 carrots, sliced
- 3 potatoes, cubed
- 1 cup of frozen or tinned garden peas
- 3 cloves of garlic, roughly chopped
- 1 litre (33fl oz) of beef stock

Simply place all of the ingredients in a casserole dish, covered. Set the oven to around 150 C/300 F and place the casserole in the centre. Cook for around 2-3 hours or until the meat is soft and tender. Make this meal go further by including the dumpling recipe from page 30.

Vegetable Stew

Like the beef recipe, this vegetable stew is a one pot recipe that serves as a stand alone meal but it doesn't require the same cooking time as the meat version, making it something you can do quickly. You can choose any vegetables you like but seasonal vegetables will always be cheaper and in my opinion, tastier.

Ingredients

- *Cauliflower florets*
- *3 - 4 potatoes, peeled and cubed*
- *½ swede/rutabega, cubed*
- *4 carrots, sliced*
- *3 onions roughly chopped*
- *2 leeks, chopped*
- *1 cup or tin of garden peas*
- *3 cloves of garlic, chopped*
- *Up to a litre (33fl oz) of vegetable stock*
- *A tablespoon of butter*

Melt the butter in a pan and saute the onions, leeks and garlic until soft. Add the stock and all of the other vegetables and turn down the heat. Leave to cook for around an hour or until the vegetables are soft. You can make this a more substantial meal by adding dumplings (page 30).

Leftover Pie

Who doesn't love pie? This version makes the most of whatever leftovers you have to hand. I often make this pie when I have a lot of leftover stew or casserole and it is as simple as rolling out the pastry and filling it before baking. You can also use whatever leftover meat or vegetables you have but you will need to add a sauce or gravy so it isn't dry.

Ingredients

- *Shortcrust pastry from page 34*
- *Leftovers*
- *Sauce or gravy if needed*

Split the pastry into two sections and roll out one of them and line a greased baking tin with it.

Fill the pastry lined tin with the filling and roll out the pastry for the pie lid on a floured surface so that it is around 0.5 cm (1/4 inch) thick. Bake in the centre of a preheated oven at 180 C /350 F for around twenty minutes. Serve with steamed vegetables.

Pasta Bake

Pasta bake can make the best of anything you've got in the fridge and needs using up.

Ingredients

- 2 cups of dried pasta
- 1 tin/can of chopped tomatoes
- 2 onions, roughly chopped
- 4 cloves of garlic, chopped
- 1 bell pepper, chopped (optional)
- 1 courgette/zucchini, sliced (optional)
- 2 carrots, diced (optional)
- 100g (4oz) grated cheese
- 1 tbsp butter

Bring a pan of salted water to the boil before adding the pasta. Turn it down to a medium heat and cook for around 10 minutes. While this is cooking, begin preparing the sauce.

In a separate pan, melt the butter and saute the onions and garlic until soft and add the pepper, courgette (zucchini) and carrot and cook for a couple of minutes. Add the tomatoes and simmer for a further five minutes.

Drain the pasta and stir in the sauce before transferring to an oven dish. Sprinkle the cheese over the top and bake in a hot oven for around 10 to 15 minutes. You can serve with a side of vegetables, meat or with garlic bread.

Toad in the Hole

This is a classic childhood recipe! Toad in the hole is simple sausages cooked in yorkshire pudding batter so that what comes from the oven is a glorious creation of yorkshire pudding with sausages encased in the base. You can use vegetarian or vegan sausages instead of meat ones for this recipe.

Ingredients

- 100g (4oz) plain flour
- 2 eggs
- 150ml (5fl oz) milk
- 8 Sausages
- 2 tbsp of oil

Preheat the oven to 200 C/390 F and start by making the batter. In a bowl, add the flour, milk and eggs and beat together until you have a smooth mixture. Place the sausages in an oven dish, drizzle with the oil and roast in the oven for around 10 minutes.

Remove the dish from the oven and pour over the batter mix. Return to the oven and cook for around 30 minutes until golden brown. Serve with potatoes and seasonal vegetables.

Vegetable Crumble

Savoury crumbles are not as common as their sweet counterparts but are utterly delicious and make a hearty evening meal. This is another of those recipes I make to use up any vegetables that are a little past their best and need using up. The beauty of this recipe is that you can use whatever vegetables you have in the fridge.

Ingredients

- 200g (7oz) plain flour
- 125g (4oz) butter
- 2 onions, roughly chopped
- 2 leeks, sliced
- 3 cloves of garlic, chopped
- 3 carrots, sliced
- ½ swede/rutabega, chopped
- cauliflower florets
- 1 cup of garden peas
- ½ butternut squash, cubed
- 2 tbsp of flour
- 2 tbsp butter
- mixed herbs
- pinch of salt
- 500ml (17fl oz) vegetable stock (page 14)

Make the crumble topping by placing the flour, butter, salt and herbs into a bowl and crumble together using your fingertips until you have a bread crumb consistency. Set to one side and melt the butter in a pan, adding the onions, leeks and garlic.

Sauté until soft and then add 2 tbsp of flour and mix in. Don't worry if it looks lumpy and weird! Add a little of the vegetable stock and mix until the flour has dissolved and the liquid is smooth, then add the rest of the stock and the vegetables and cook for five minutes. Transfer to an oven dish and add the crumble topping. Bake for around 25 minutes at 180 C / 350 F and serve.

Chapter 4
Easy Meals

I love cooking but sometimes, especially after coming home after a day at work, I just cannot be bothered to make a fancy meal but still want something tasty and relatively healthy to tuck into. This section contains some of my favourite meals that take less than an hour to make, prep time and all!

Sausage Casserole

Unlike other casseroles, sausage casserole doesn't take as long to cook and can be prepared, cooked and served within the hour, making a delicious home cooked meal. You can easily substitute meat sausages for veggie or vegan ones if you need to.

Ingredients

- *6 - 8 sausages*
- *2 onions, roughly chopped*
- *2 carrots, sliced*
- *1 -2 bell peppers, sliced*
- *2 - 3 cloves of garlic, finely chopped or crushed*
- *2 tbsp oil*
- *2 tbsp flour*
- *400ml (13fl oz) vegetable stock. (page 14)*

In a large pan, heat the oil over a medium heat and add the sausages, cooking for around five minutes until the skin is browned. Remove from the pan and add the onions, garlic and peppers and sauté for a few minutes until soft. Add the flour and mix in. Do not worry if it looks lumpy, this is perfectly normal.

Add the vegetable stock slowly, continuously mixing until the liquid is smooth and silky with the flour dissolved. Return the sausages to the pan and add the carrots before simmering for around 30 minutes until the carrots are soft and the sausages cooked through.

Corned Beef Hash

A working class staple, corned beef hash has fallen out of fashion in recent years and yet this is an easy and extremely cheap meal. I used to make this quite often for my family when money was tight (and by tight, I mean we had none!)

Ingredients

- 1 tin corned beef, cut into cubes
- 2 tbsp butter
- 2 onions, roughly chopped
- 3 potatoes, cubed and boiled
- 3 carrots, chopped and parboiled
- 2 garlic cloves, finely chopped or minced
- Eggs - 1 for each serving
- Herbs for seasoning (those you like or have available)
- Salt and pepper

Melt the butter in a large pan over a medium heat and saute the onions and garlic until soft. Add the corned beef, potatoes and carrots and cook for a further 10 minutes, stirring occasionally. Add herbs, salt and pepper to taste. While this is cooking, heat a pan of water and poach one egg per person. Serve the egg on top of the hash and enjoy.

You can make this meal go further by adding extra potatoes and vegetables.

Savoury Bread & Butter Pudding

A proper old school dish, savoury bread and butter pudding is delicious and so easy and quick to make. It's a great way of using up stale bread or bread just past its use-by date, so long as it doesn't have mould on it. You will need:

Ingredients

- *6 slices of bread cut into triangles*
- *400ml (14fl oz) milk*
- *3 eggs*
- *1 onion, finely chopped*
- *50g (2 oz) cheese, grated*
- *bacon or ham, chopped (optional)*

Grease a baking tray or casserole dish and line it with the bread. Build the layers up until you have used all the bread. Sprinkle the chopped onion and bacon or ham evenly over the bread before doing the same with the cheese. Beat the eggs into the milk and pour evenly over the layered bread, onions, cheese, and meat.

Cook at 180 C /350 F for around twenty minutes or until cooked. Serve with steamed vegetables or beans.

Cheese & Onion Quiche

This recipe makes use of the basic shortcrust pastry (page 34). You can make a batch of this up and freeze it but it really doesn't take long to make at all. If you want a meaty version then you can add bacon pieces or lardons.

Ingredients

- *Shortcrust pastry, enough to line a deep sided baking tray*
- *4 eggs, beaten*
- *50ml milk*
- *1 onion, roughly chopped*
- *150g (5oz) of grated cheese*
- *Butter for greasing the tray*

Grease the baking tray and roll out the pastry until it is roughly around 1/2 cm (1/4 inch) thick and line the tray. Add the onions and the cheese. Mix the milk with the eggs and pour the mixture over the cheese and onions and place the quiche in the centre of a hot oven (180 C/ 350 F) and bake for around 20 to 25 minutes until the eggs have risen and solidified. Serve with salad or potatoes and garden peas.

Omelet

Omelets are so very versatile, healthy, and if you fill it with plenty of good stuff can be part of a main meal. This is another one of those recipes where you can add whatever you have in your fridge. If you are going to use potatoes, then I suggest parboiling them as there is nothing worse than having hard potatoes or burnt omelet! Other than that, let your own personal tastes lead the way.

Ingredients

- *4 eggs, beaten*
- *1 potato, thinly sliced or cut or cubed and parboiled*
- *1 onion, sliced*
- *1 garlic clove, finely chopped*
- *1 large tomato, chopped or a handful of cherry tomatoes, halved*
- *1 bell pepper, chopped*
- *100g (4oz) grated cheese*
- *1 tbsp butter*

Heat the butter in a large frying pan and add the egg mixture, adding all of the vegetables. Cook until the bottom has firmed up and add the cheese. Cover the pan and lower the heat. Leave until the egg has cooked thoroughly and serve with salad.

Spaghetti Bolognese

This is one of my go to meals for when I want something quick. You can use beef or a vegetarian alternative.

Ingredients

- Enough pasta or spaghetti for the number of people
- 400g (14oz) minced/ground beef
- 2 onions, chopped
- 4 cloves of garlic, chopped
- 300ml (10oz) tomato sauce (page 21)
- 2 bell peppers, chopped
- (optional) 1 chopped carrot
- Mixed herbs
- 200ml (7fl oz) of beef stock
- 100g (4oz) grated cheese
- herbs (oregano or basil)
- (optional): 6 juniper berries

Bring a pan of salted water to the boil and add the pasta or spaghetti, turning down to a medium heat. In a large pan, add the minced beef and onions. If you are using full fat beef, you will not need extra oil. Brown the mince with the onions and add the garlic, carrot (optional), and peppers. Cook for a couple of minutes before adding the tomato sauce, the beef stock and the herbs. Cook over a medium heat until the sauce has thickened, this normally takes around ten minutes, by which time the pasta should be cooked. Serve with grated cheese.

Spicy Couscous

I always feel that couscous is one of those underrated ingredients. It is so very versatile and is super easy and quick to make. I love a bit of spice in my food because it is an easy way of adding flavour, jazzing up the most basic of meals.

Ingredients

- *1 cup of couscous*
- *1 ½ cups of water*
- *1 tbsp butter*
- *1 hot chilli pepper, deseeded and chopped*
- *1 onion finely chopped*
- *2 cloves of garlic*
- *1 bell pepper, chopped*
- *½ cup of garden peas*
- *Sprig of thyme*
- *Pinch of salt*

Bring the water to the boil and add the salt, thyme and butter before adding the couscous. Cook for a minute, stirring continuously before removing from the heat. Cover with the lid and let stand for five minutes. Meanwhile, heat a little butter in a pan and saute the onion, garlic, chilli pepper and pepper until soft. Add to the couscous and mix in. Serve with seasonal vegetables. If you eat meat, you can always add bacon lardons or sliced sausages.

Roast Vegetables with a Baked Egg

This is a good way of using up vegetables that are just past their best.

Ingredients

- 2- 3 onions, quartered
- 3 carrots, chopped
- Squash or pumpkin, peeled and chopped
- Bell peppers cut into strips
- 2 courgettes/zucchini, chopped
- 2-3 potatoes, peeled and chopped
- 4 eggs
- Salt & pepper for seasoning
- Chilli flakes
- 1 tsp paprika
- 1 tbsp cooking oil

Place all of the vegetables in a large bowl and drizzle with the oil, adding the salt, pepper, paprika, and chilli flakes before giving them a good toss, ensuring the vegetables are evenly covered. Transfer to a baking tray and roast in the centre of the oven at around 180 C/350 F. After 15 minutes, remove the tray from the oven and crack the eggs over the vegetables before returning to the oven for another 15 minutes or until the eggs have cooked and the vegetables are soft.

Easy Chicken & Rice

This is a very easy and nutritious meal. If you can, prepare the chicken the night before and leave to marinate overnight. Don't worry if you just don't have the time to do it, it will still be delicious.

Ingredients

- *400g (14oz) chicken thighs and drumsticks*
- *4 or 5 scallions/green onions, including the green parts*
- *4 garlic cloves, finely chopped*
- *1 tbsp thyme*
- *1 tbsp ground allspice*
- *2 chilli peppers chopped (adjust to suit your own tastes)*
- *2 cups of rice*
- *3 cups of chicken or vegetable stock*
- *A knob of butter (about 2 tbsp)*
- *Salt*
- *1 tbsp cooking oil*

Prepare the chicken by placing it in a large bowl along with the scallions, garlic, thyme, allspice, peppers and a pinch of salt and mix together so that the chicken is evenly covered. Leave in the fridge overnight or for a couple of hours if time permits. Turn out onto a roasting tin and drizzle with oil before cooking in the centre of a hot oven at 180C/ 350F for thirty minutes or until cooked.

While the chicken is cooking in the oven, start on the rice. Place the stock in a pot along with the butter and bring to the boil before turning down to a medium heat. While the stock heats up, wash the rice under running water until the water runs clear. Add to the stock and place the lid on. Cook for around five minutes then remove from the heat and leave the lid on for around ten minutes. Do not be tempted to take the lid off to check the rice. After ten minutes has passed, remove the lid and fluff the rice using a fork. Serve with the chicken along with a side salad.

Easy Vegetable Curry

I love Indian cuisine, the flavours are simply divine. However if you've ever tried to cook a curry from scratch, the spice list alone can be enough to put you off trying, indeed there is a real skill in flavouring a curry just so, getting the perfect ratio of spices. Sometimes, when I come in from a long day at work and fancy an easy curry, one that won't take too long to make, I use this recipe.

Ingredients

- 2 onions, roughly chopped
- 3 carrots, sliced
- pumpkin or squash, peeled and cubed
- 2 bell peppers, chopped
- 3 cloves of garlic, chopped
- 1 tin chopped tomatoes
- 1 tbsp tomato puree
- 2 cups of vegetable stock
- 2 tbsp hot curry powder
- ½ tsp ground ginger
- 1 tbsp oil

Heat the oil in a large pan and cook the onions and garlic until soft before adding the rest of the vegetables along with the chopped tomatoes and vegetable stock. Add the curry powder and ginger along with the tomato puree, and cook for around 15 minutes, stirring occasionally until the liquid has reduced and the vegetables are cooked. Serve with rice.

Pasta, Peas & Bacon With A Cheese Sauce

When my oldest son was young, he was a very fussy eater but he would always eat this meal. This is cheap to make and you can use less or more bacon depending on how much you have available.

Ingredients

- 300ml basic white sauce (page 19)
- 2 cups dry pasta
- Bacon lardons or slices that have been chopped
- 100g (4oz) grated cheese
- 1 tbsp butter

Bring a pot of water to the boil before adding the pasta and turning to a medium heat, cooking for ten minutes. While the pasta cooks, in another pan, melt the butter and cook the bacon for a couple of minutes. Add the white sauce and the cheese and stir continuously until the cheese has melted. Drain the water for the pasta and stir in the sauce. Serve with garlic bread.

Chapter 5
Snacks & Sides

Sometimes we don't want a massive meal. Sometimes a snack will do. Other times we might just want a little something to go with a side of salad or to compliment a main meal. The recipes in this section will do as a snack or as part of a bigger meal. These are super easy to make but delicious nonetheless and cheap too.

Veggie Peel Crisps

Ingredients

Vegetable peelings are often discarded either on the compost heap or in the bin but they can make a tasty treat and a nice alternative to shop-bought crisps or chips. I often make these and they never last long! You can flavour them however you like but my go-to flavouring is salt, pepper, paprika and chilli powder. You can use such a wide range of vegetable peel as well including potato, squash, carrot, beetroot and many more. To make these you will need:

Ingredients

- *Cooking oil*
- *Vegetable peels*
- *Seasoning of your choice.*

Heat the oil in a large pan and deep fry the peel for a few minutes. You can tell when it is done as the crisps will begin to float. Remove from the pan and allow to drain before seasoning. It is as easy as that!

Bubble & Squeak

This is one of my favourite things to eat, either as supper or as part of a full English breakfast. Bubble and squeak is proper peasant food but very delicious. It is traditionally made from cooked potatoes and cabbage, the leftovers from a Sunday lunch. You can just keep it to the classics but I tend to make it with the potatoes and any other leftover veg from a roast dinner. Here I will give the classic recipe

Ingredients

- *Leftover boiled potatoes, crushed*
- *Leftover steamed cabbage*
- *1 onion finely chopped*
- *2 tbsp oil for frying*
- *Pinch of salt*

Heat the oil in a large frying pan or skillet. In a bowl mix the crushed or mashed potatoes, cabbage, onions and salt. Form into small patties and fry on each side until golden. Serve as part of a full English breakfast. I like them on their own topped with a little grated cheese.

Baked Egg Bread & Cheese

I make this all the time as a quick and easy lunch and my family love it. It is so basic to make but seems like a treat. This recipe is for a single serving and often I'll just do one slice if it's part of a larger meal or two for a filling lunch that will last through to tea time.

Ingredients

- *1 slice of bread, buttered*
- *1 egg*
- *Grated cheese*

Preheat the oven to 180 C/350 F. Place the slice of bread on a baking tray and using the back of a tablespoon, press down the centre of the bread until it has a shallow well in it. Break the egg in this well and sprinkle the cheese around the edge of the bread. Bake in the oven for around 15 to 20 minutes until the egg is cooked.

Fancy Garlic Baguette

This is another one of those dishes that make the most of what you have got in the fridge and can be served as a lunchtime meal in itself.

Ingredients

- *A garlic or regular baguette*
- *½ onion, chopped*
- *½ bell pepper, chopped*
- *A handful of cherry tomatoes, halved*
- *Cooked ham, diced*
- *Grated cheese*

Preheat the oven. Take the baguette and cut it down its length making sure to not cut through it completely. Fill the baguette with the chopped onion, tomatoes, peppers and ham and sprinkle with the grated cheese. Bake in the oven for around 15 minutes and serve with a salad. You can also serve with bolognese or chilli as a way to make the meal go even further.

Sauteed Garden Peas

I love garden peas and for this recipe you can use tinned or frozen. It is a real country dish and is the perfect accompaniment to any meal or as a light meal served with fresh crusty bread, toasted and buttered.

Ingredients

- *Tin/can of garden peas or 100g of frozen peas*
- *2 cloves of garlic, finely chopped*
- *½ onion, finely chopped*
- *2 tbsp butter*
- *Squeeze of lemon*
- *Salt & pepper*
- *Sprig of thyme*

Melt the butter in a pan and saute the onion and garlic until soft. Add the peas and cook for around 4 minutes. Add a squeeze of lemon juice along with the salt, pepper and thyme. Serve with crusty bread freshly toasted or as a side to a larger meal.

Stuffed Peppers

You can stuff peppers with almost anything and they are a good way to fill out a basic salad. For a vegetarian option, leave out the meat. This serves two people.

Ingredients

- 2 bell peppers
- 1 onion, chopped
- 3 cloves of garlic, chopped
- ½ tin of mixed bean salad
- Cooked ham, diced
- 1 chilli pepper, finely chopped
- Grate cheese
- 1 tsp paprika
- Salt & pepper

Preheat the oven to 180 C/350 F. Take a bowl and add the onions, garlic, bean salad, meat and chilli pepper along with the salt, pepper and paprika. Mix thoroughly. Take the peppers and carefully slice off the tops. Stand them on a baking tray (I use my yorkshire pudding tin so the peppers don't topple over as they begin to cook, but a large muffin tin would also work) and fill with the mixture, sprinkling the cheese on top. Bake in the oven for around ten minutes and serve while still warm.

Roast Chickpeas

If you don't like chickpeas, then you can substitute them for another type of bean (I recommend broad beans or french peas).

Ingredients

- *1 tin of chickpeas, drained*
- *1 onion, chopped*
- *2 cloves of garlic*
- *1 chilli pepper*
- *1 tsp paprika*
- *Rosemary*
- *2 tbsp oil*

Combine all of the ingredients in a large bowl and mix thoroughly before turning out onto a baking tray. Cook in the centre of a hot oven for ten minutes. Serve as a side to a larger meal or with a salad.

Cauliflower Gratin

One of my favourites, cauliflower gratin is a great addition to any meal, transforming the most ordinary into something decadent.. I suggest using a mature cheddar, as strong as you like it so you get that hit of flavour but you can use any cheese you have or prefer.

Ingredients

- *1 cauliflower, cut into pieces*
- *500ml (17fl oz) milk*
- *100g (4oz) cheese*
- *50g (2oz) butter*
- *4 tbsp flour*
- *Pepper to season*

Place the cauliflower in a pot of salted water and bring to the boil before turning down to a medium heat. Allow to cook for five minutes before removing from the heat. Drain the liquid and spread the cauliflower out in an ovenproof dish.

Next, add the milk, butter and flour into a saucepan and bring to the boil, whisking continuously until the liquid begins to thicken. Keep on whisking until you have a thick and creamy sauce. Remove the pan from the heat and add the cheese, mixing it in until it has melted. Pour the sauce over the cauliflower, add the pepper and bake at 200 C/ 375 F for around twenty minutes. Serve as a side dish to enhance the most basic of meals.

Savoury Pancakes

In the UK, pancakes are mostly a sweet treat. When I was a kid, the best way to have pancakes was still warm with squeezed orange juice and sugar but nowadays I prefer these savoury pancakes. They make a nice lunch or can be served as part of a larger meal. You will need:

Ingredients

- 1 cup of plain flour
- 1 cup of milk
- 1 egg
- 1 onion, chopped
- 1 clove of garlic 3 tbsp butter for cooking
- 100g (4oz) grated cheese

To begin, make the batter for the pancakes by mixing together the flour, milk and egg until you have a smooth batter mix. Set to one side and take a small frying pan and saute the onion and garlic in 1 tbsp of butter until soft and empty in a bowl. Using the same pan, add 1 tbsp butter and melt before pouring in some of the batter mix. Cook until the batter begins to solidify on the top and flip over, cooking for another minute or two until golden brown. Slide onto a plate and add some of the garlic and onion before adding 2 tbsp of grated cheese. Fold the pancake in half and add to the pan for another minute or two so that the cheese melts. Repeat until you have used the batter.

Chutney

Chutney is a great way of using up those vegetables that are past their best and perhaps soft to the touch. They are also good to make if you have a lot of produce and are not sure what to do with it and can jazz up the most boring of sandwiches. This is a basic chutney recipe so don't be afraid to make any substitutions you see fit.

Ingredients

- 2 kg (70oz) of tomatoes (either ripe or green tomatoes) peeled and chopped
- 400g (14oz) of apples peeled and chopped
- 240g (8oz) onions chopped
- 330g (12oz) sugar
- 1.25 (35fl oz) litres malt vinegar
- 1 tsp ground ginger
- ½ tsp cinnamon
- ½ tsp ground cloves

Place all of the ingredients into a large pan and stir over a medium heat until the sugar has completely dissolved before bringing to the boil. Turn to a medium heat and allow the mixture to simmer for around an hour and thirty minutes or until it is thick, stirring occasionally. Spoon into hot sterilised jars and seal while hot.

Chapter 6
Wild Eats

If you've ever been out blackberry picking, then you have foraged. While fruits are the obvious choice for wild food, there is so much you can eat that grows on your doorstep! It should go without saying that if you do decide to forage for food, to be mindful of the area you are harvesting from, to take only what you need, leaving more than enough for the other beings that rely on that space for shelter and food. It's also worth pointing out to be mindful of where you are foraging from as well and you'd do well to avoid taking plants from common dog walking areas! If you can, try not to pick plants and foods that grow by busy roadsides as traffic pollution can contaminate more than just the surface. Common weeds and invasive species are always going to be in plentiful supply and you might just be surprised at how good they taste too.

What I love most about foraging, beside the connection to the land where I live, is the ability to go outside and return with something I can make a delicious meal with.

Sauteed Dandelion Stems & Leaves

There's been more than once where my family have eaten foraged greens without even knowing! For some folks, there is a reluctance about eating wild greens, that is dandelion leaf and stem, red clover, nasturtium and others. Perhaps this reluctance stems from our reliance on vegetables that have been neatly preened and packaged.

This recipe makes use of dandelion stems and leaves. Dandelions grow in abundance and if harvested with care and thought to the other creatures we share this world with, can be a good way of introducing foraged foods into your own diet.

Ingredients

- Dandelion stems and leaves, roughly chopped
- 3 cloves of garlic, finely chopped
- ½ onion, finely chopped
- 2 tbsp butter for cooking

Melt the butter in a pan over a medium heat and add the onions and garlic, cooking until soft. Add the dandelion stems and cook for a couple of minutes before adding the leaves and cooing for a further two minutes. Serve as a side dish to a larger meal. Alternatively top with a little grated cheese and serve with toast.

Watercress Soup

Ingredients

- 2 onions, chopped
- 2 celery sticks, chopped
- 4 potatoes, cubed
- 3 cloves of garlic
- 100g (4oz) watercress
- 600ml (20fl oz) vegetable or chicken stock
- 2tbsp butter
- Salt & pepper
- Sprig of thyme

Melt the butter in a large pan over a medium heat and add the onions, garlic and celery. Cook for a few minutes until softened and add the stock along with the potatoes. Bring to the boil before allowing to simmer for 15 minutes before adding the watercress and along with the thyme and salt and pepper. Cook for another 15 minutes before removing from the heat and blending until smooth. Serve with buttered bread and enjoy!

Nettle Soup

This recipe is so very simple and nutritious as well. Pick nettles when young else they begin to taste bitter and can be tough.

Ingredients

- *2 onions, roughly chopped*
- *1 leek, chopped*
- *3-4 cloves of garlic, chopped*
- *1 large potato, cubed*
- *2 carrots, sliced*
- *200g (8oz) nettle leaves, washed*
- *600ml (20fl oz) vegetable or chicken stock*
- *50ml of double cream*
- *2tbsp butter*
- *Salt & pepper*

Melt the butter in a pan and saute the onions, leek and garlic until soft. Add the carrots and cook for a further 2 minutes before adding the stock along with the potatoes. Cook until the potatoes begin to soften and then add the nettle leaves. Cook for a further five to ten minutes before removing from the heat and blending. Stir in the cream and season to taste.

Stewed Rabbit

When it comes to rabbit, wild rabbit will always be a better option than farmed rabbit. Whatever the meat, modern factory farming is crueler to the animal both in terms of welfare and slaughter. A good shot with a rifle is so much kinder if you want a little meat in your diet.

The key to cooking rabbit is to cook it long and slow, especially if you are not overly fond of the gamey taste. If you are inexperienced with butchering a rabbit then take it to your local butchers who will happily joint it for you.

Ingredients

- *Rabbit, jointed*
- *1 litre (34fl oz) of meat stock*
- *2 onions, chopped*
- *3 garlic cloves, chopped*
- *2 leeks, chopped*
- *3 carrots, sliced*
- *Sprig of rosemary*
- *2tbsp oil for browning*
- *2tbsp plain flour*
- *Salt & pepper for seasoning*

Heat the oil in a frying pan and brown the meat before transferring to a large pan along with the stock and cook on a medium heat. In the frying pan, cook the onions, garlic, carrots and leek for a few minutes until soft. Add the flour to the vegetables and just mix in. Don't worry if it looks messy as the flour will nicely thicken the stew as it cooks. Add the floured vegetables to the rabbit and stock along with the rosemary and the salt and pepper. Turn the heat down low and allow the stew to cook slowly for around 2-3 hours until the meat comes away from the bone. Serve with potatoes or remove the bones and make a pie using the pastry recipe (page 34).

Pan Roasted Cobnuts

Cobnuts are the wild variety of hazel nuts and they grow all over my small town! I forage for these in the autumn and they make a great alternative to crisps (chips for US folks). If cobnuts do not grow near you then you can use any kind of nut you like the taste of.

Ingredients

- *1 cup of nuts, deshelled*
- *1 tbsp of oil of your choice or butter*
- *Salt and pepper to taste*

Melt the butter or heat the oil in a frying pan over a medium heat. Add the nuts and cook for around five minutes, rolling the pan every so often to get a nice even colouring. Remove from the heat and season with salt and pepper to taste. Eat while still warm.

Elderflower Fritters

Elderflowers are so delightfully delicious and are so much more than a trendy mixer for your alcoholic drinks. These fritters make a light treat and are so quick and easy to make.

Ingredients

- *3 cups elderflower flowers, removed from the stalk and lightly rinsed and drained*
- *1 cup plain flour*
- *½ cup water*
- *½ cup milk*
- *Pinch salt*
- *1 tsp sugar*
- *Oil for (deep) frying.*
- *Icing sugar for dusting*

Heat the oil in a large pan on a medium to high heat. While the oil heats up, prepare the batter by mixing the flour, water, milk, sugar and salt into a large bowl, whisking until the batter is silky smooth. Next, add the flowers to the batter. And mix in so that all of the flowers are covered. When the oil is hot, add dollops of the batter mixture to the frying pan, cooking for a couple of minutes on each side until the batter is a light golden brown. Remove from the pan and allow to drain before dusting with icing sugar. Enjoy while still warm.

Rosehip, Crabapple & Haw Jelly

This is the perfect autumnal recipe and what I love about it is the fact you can go out for a lovely walk and collect the ingredients at the same time! For this recipe you will need:

Ingredients

- 1kg rowan berries & rosehips combined
- 500g crab apples peeled and roughly chopped
- Sugar

To begin, remove the rowan berries and rosehips from their stalks and place in a pan with the peeled and chopped crab apples and add enough water so that the fruit is just covered. Bring to the boil before turning the heat down and allowing to simmer, stirring the fruit occasionally and using the back of the spoon to push the fruit against the side of the pan so that as much juice as possible is extracted.

Strain using a sieve or preferably a clean cotton or muslin cloth, squeezing as much of the juice as possible from the mixture. You will need to measure how much juice you have as this will determine how much sugar you will need to use. For every litre of juice, you will need to add 750g of sugar. Place into a clean pan and stir over a gentle heat until the sugar has fully dissolved before boiling quickly. You can use a kitchen thermometer to determine when the mixture is ready, but I don't have one so what I do is place a small plate in the fridge until it is cold and then drip a little of the mixture onto it. If, after a few seconds, it doesn't run and the top crinkles when prodded, your mixture is ready. Remove the mixture from the heat and spoon into hot sterilised jars. You can leave for a few weeks to mature and will keep for up to a year if stored correctly.

Violet Honey

To be fair, you can flavour honey with whatever edible flowers you like such as lavender but violet honey is my absolute favourite. There's nothing quite like going out and picking beautiful, fresh wild violets (always making sure you don't decimate an area, taking only what you need) and using them to flavour honey.

I make this in small amounts as a treat which helps ensure I'm not over harvesting the violets that grow in my garden.

To make violet honey simply collect violets and give them a quick rinse under a light flow of water. Place them in a clean jar before adding the honey. Leave on a warm windowsill for a week before using. If you wish, you can strain the honey out and discard the flowers but I just eat them too!

Crystallised Flowers

These delicious floral treats add a touch of magic to any dessert or can be enjoyed on their own. To make crystallised flowers, you will need:

Ingredients

- *Edible flowers of your choice, though violets are a favourite of mine.*
- *100g (4oz) sugar*
- *2 tbsp water*

Put the sugar and water in a pan turn on the heat, stirring continuously until the sugar has melted and you have a syrup. Be careful not to let it burn or caramelise.

Remove from the heat, and working quickly before the sugar begins to set, place the flowers in the sugar so they are thoroughly covered and then place on a baking sheet until the sugar sets. Keep in a clean jar.

Blackberry Jam

This is another of those recipes where you can forage the ingredients. Picking juicy blackberries on a late summer's day is a glorious way to spend some time getting closer to nature and if you have children, you get to spend some quality time with them outdoors too.

Blackberries grow in abundance and so if you are worried about the effects of foraging on your local landscape, then you can pick a few safe in the knowledge that there are more than enough blackberries for you and for the wildlife you share the world with.

This is a very basic jam recipe that uses equal amounts of fruit and sugar. To make enough for a couple of jars of jam, you will need:

- *500g (18oz) blackberries*
- *500g sugar*
- *Juice of 1 lemon*
- *50ml (2fl oz) water*

Place the blackberries and the water in a pan along with the sugar and the lemon juice and heat gently, being careful not to boil until the sugar has dissolved. Bring the mixture to a rolling boil for 10 minutes before lowering the heat and simmering for around 30 minutes, stirring occasionally.

To test the consistency of the jam, allow a few droplets to fall onto a cold plate. If they run, then the mixture needs a little longer on the heat. When the jam is ready, pour into clean sterilized jars while still hot. You can either add the lids while the jam is piping hot or wait until they have cooled right down to room temperature.

Wild Flower Cordial

Flower cordials are so luxurious. Sipping one of these on a sunny afternoon with a good book beneath a tree is my idea of heaven. As extravagant as they sound, fruit cordials are both easy and pretty cheap to make. While they do have a high sugar content, diluted and poured over ice they make a refreshing and hydrating drink. Some of my favourite flowers to use are violet, elderflower, and flowering currant.

Whichever you decide to use, do take care when foraging for ingredients, making sure to take only what you need and only when there is a plentiful supply. Growing edible flowers yourself is a good alternative if you have the space and are able to.

Ingredients

- 1.5 litre (34fl oz) water
- 1kg (35oz) sugar
- 5 cups flowers of your choice

Make sure you have trimmed as much of the stems off the flowers as possible and rinse lightly under running water. Combine the water and the flowers in a large pan and simmer on a gentle heat for around 45 minutes. Strain the liquid into a clean pan and add the sugar before returning to a gentle heat, stirring continuously. When the sugar has fully dissolved, turn off the heat and allow the liquid to cool before pouring into a clean bottle. Refrigerate and use as needed.

Elderflower Wine

Wine making is so much easier than people think! Elderflower wine is one of my all time favourite tipples. It has a sweet, floral taste that reminds me of springtime sunshine.

Ingredients

- Elderflowers, enough to fill a medium sized pan
- 2 litres (67fl oz) of water
- The juice and zest of one lemon or orange
- 2 teaspoons of ordinary dried baker's yeast (you can buy special wine making yeast but if I'm honest, I can't taste the difference between the two).
- 1kg (35oz) of caster sugar (again you can use ordinary granulated sugar but it just takes a little longer to dissolve).

To begin, you will need to prepare the flowers by cutting away as much of the stem as possible. This can be a little tiresome with elderflowers because each spray has so many but it is worth the effort. You might be tempted to wash the flowers but don't. Place them in a large pot and fill with water so that the flowers are just covered and bring to the boil before turning the heat down and allowing to simmer for around an hour. Don't let the pot go dry and keep topping up with water. After, turn the heat off and leave the flowers to sit in the water for around a day or two. Strain into a large por or sterilized bucket and add more water until you have 2 litres of liquid.

Fill a separate pot with two litres of water and add the sugar, heating the mixture slowly and stirring continuously until the sugar has dissolved. Add the lemon or orange zest and juice to this mixture then add the whole lot to the flower water. Now empty the yeast into a bowl and add a little water. When it starts bubbling, add it to the flower syrup and stir in.

Then transfer the liquid into a demijohn and fit with an airlock. This allows the gases produced by the fermentation process to escape. You'll know when it begins to ferment because it will bubble and foam. This can take anywhere between 2 and 6 months.

When it's finished fermenting (when it's stopped bubbling and releasing gas), then it's time to carefully syphon the wine into another demijohn or bottle, making sure you leave behind any sediment. Leave to stand again for a month and syphon off again. If you want to repeat this step then do so otherwise it's time to bottle up your wine. Now the longer you leave the wine to mature, the better it will taste but I'm impatient and have to try at least one bottle! Be warned though, this wine can be pretty potent and if it is too strong then you can dilute it by adding lemonade or sparkling water to your glass. Enjoy!

Blackberry & Elderberry Wine

The process of wine making is pretty much the same no matter the type of wine; however when making wine using fruits, there is a slight adaptation concerning how you prepare the fruit. Blackberry and elderberry wine is the perfect summer berry combination and spending the day out of doors picking berries is a great way to get the family out in the fresh air.

Ingredients

- 2kg (70oz) blackberries and elderberries
- The juice and zest of a lemon or orange
- 1kg (35oz) caster sugar
- 2 (67fl oz) litres water
- 2 teaspoons of baker's yeast

To prepare the berries, tidy them up by removing any stalks but do not wash. Place in a large pan with 2 litres of water and bring to the boil before turning the heat down. Allow to simmer and as it does so, with a spatula or back of a serving spoon or ladle, agitate the berries and press against the side of the pan. Allow to cool and then strain into a large pan or sterilized bucket using a clean piece of muslin to catch the berries.

Squeeze as much juice from the berries as possible and leave the liquid to stand for a day or two then simply follow the processes from the previous recipe by then preparing the sugar syrup and getting the yeast ready.

Infused Spirits

Infusing or flavouring alcohol with fruits is a great way of using those fruits that are perhaps a little overripe or bruised and is an old country tradition. You've probably heard of sloe gin, that is gin infused with sloes, the fruit of the blackthorn (and about the only real use for the bitter tasting fruits), but cherry brandy is also a favourite of mine (also, nobody in my house likes cherry jam or pie and with two cherry trees in my garden, well, why not?)

Infusing spirits is so easy: you literally need the fruits and a bottle of spirits such as brandy, rum, gin, or vodka. The more fruits you use, the stronger the flavour will be, and it is often a good idea to freeze the fruits before using as this causes the skins to split and so allows the juice and flavours to be extracted more fully.

To make infused spirits, place the fruits in a demijohn or large bottle and pour over the alcohol. I don't give any measures here but you will want to make sure the alcohol covers the fruits completely so they do not go mouldy. Add a lid and leave for at least two weeks before straining the alcohol into a clean bottle.

Chapter 7
Sweet Eats

Easy Custard

Don't let anyone tell you custard is difficult to make...it isn't! Most custard recipes call for the use of cream but there have been plenty of times when I've been skint and so have used milk and it tastes just as good. To make custard, you will need:

- *400ml (14fl oz) milk*
- *2 eggs*
- *1 teaspoon vanilla extract*
- *2tbsp sugar*

Heat the milk in a pan along with the vanilla extract and remove from the heat just as it begins to boil. While it cools down, beat the eggs and the sugar together. If using cream then I'd suggest just using the yolks of the eggs, but because we are using just milk, we'll include the whites as well.

Now is the risky part, pouring the warm milk over the eggs. Stir continuously with a spoon to avoid scrambling the eggs. Pour through a sieve back into the pan and add to the heat once more, stirring continuously until the sugar has dissolved and the custard is at the desired consistency.

Basic Sponge Recipe

There's something about a moist sponge cake that makes the most simple of suppers seem like a feast. This basic sponge recipe is easy and often forms the basis for many of my own cakes. You will need:

- *150g (5oz) self raising flour*
- *150g (5oz) sugar*
- *150g (5oz) butter*
- *3 eggs*
- *50ml (2fl oz) milk*

Preheat the oven to 180 C/ 375 F. Cream the butter and sugar together and then add the eggs and milk, beating them in. Don't worry if the mixture looks curdled at this point, it's supposed to! Slowly add the flour, mixing it in until you have a smooth cake batter. Pour into a lined or greased baking tin and bake in the centre of the oven for around 30 minutes. Check the cake is cooked by inserting a fork into the centre. If it comes out clean, then the cake is cooked. Serve with custard.

You can also make small individual cupcakes using the same mixture and cooking for around 12 minutes at the same temperature.

Ginger Cake

Growing up, I would have ginger cake at my grandparents house and so this cake brings back cozy memories. This builds on spongecake recipe.

-
- *150g (5oz) self raising flour*
- *150g (5oz) sugar*
- *150g (5oz) butter*
- *3 eggs*
- *50ml (2fl oz) milk*
- *1 tbsp ground ginger (you can add more or less depending on your own personal tastes)*
- *1 tsp cinnamon*
- *Golden syrup*

Preheat the oven to 180 degrees. Cream the butter and sugar together and then add the eggs and milk, beating them in. Don't worry if the mixture looks curdled at this point, it's supposed to! Combine the ginger, cinnamon and flour and slowly add to the butter, sugar, eggs and milk until you have a smooth cake batter. Pour into a lined or greased baking tin and bake in the centre of the oven for around 30 minutes. Check the cake is cooked by inserting a fork into the centre. If it comes out clean, then the cake is cooked. Remove from the oven and using a fork, poke holes into the cake and then drizzle with the golden syrup, allowing it to soak in. Serve with custard or ice cream

Jumble Cake

This is one of those things that takes me straight back to my childhood. I don't know if my mum thought this up or whether it is an actual recipe from somewhere else, but when my sisters and I were kids, my mum would make jumble cake, so called because it was a jumble of ingredients thrown together.

I guess really it was a basic sponge with added extras depending on what we had in the cupboard. It was usually a multicoloured affair, sometimes with icing, other times with raisins, sometimes just a plain sponge which we'd have with custard. Whatever was in it, I loved it!

To make your own jumble cake, use the plain sponge recipe (page x) and add whatever you like or have, including soft fruits, raisins, food colourings, icing, or whatever!

Banana Bread

Once bananas go brown, a lot of people are put off eating them, though they are often still good. Instead of throwing them away, I bake banana bread with them. This recipe is very basic and if you want to add walnuts or sultanas (yellow raisings) you can.

- *3 or 4 overripe bananas, mashed*
- *200g (7oz) of self raising flour*
- *150g (5oz) sugar*
- *150g (5oz) butter*
- *3 eggs, beaten*
- *2 tbsp milk*

Preheat the oven to 180C/ 375C and in a bowl mix the butter and the sugar until it is creamy and then add the eggs, and milk, mixing them in. Slowly add the flour and mix together before pouring into a greased or lined loaf tin.

Bake in the centre of the oven for around 30 minutes or until cooked thoroughly. You can check whether it is baked through by inserting a fork into the centre. If it comes out clean then the cake is cooked. Remove from the oven and allow to cool.

Butter Biscuits

Biscuits are relatively cheap to buy but nothing shop-bought beats these delicious butter biscuits. To make these you will need:

- *150g (5oz) plain flour*
- *100g (4oz) butter*
- *50g sugar*

Preheat the oven to 180 degrees and grease or line a baking tray. In a bowl, beat the butter so that it softens and slowly add the sugar, creaming them together. Add the flour to form a dough. Divide the mixture into around 12 even sizes and shape them into balls.

Place them on the baking tray and push down on the balls of dough to slightly flatten them. Cook in the middle of a hot oven for around 10 - 15 minutes. Remove from the oven and allow to cool.

Frozen Fruit Yoghurt

This is a really simple dessert and can be made cheaply. You can buy natural yoghurt, unbranded or store-brand varieties for so much less than their branded counterparts.

Ingredients

- 300g (11oz) natural yoghurt
- 100g (4oz) soft fruit such as strawberries
- 1 tbsp caster sugar.

In a bowl combine the fruit and the sugar and, using a fork, mash up the fruit, mixing in with the sugar. When you are happy with the consistency add the natural yoghurt and mix thoroughly. Place the yoghurt mixture into containers suitable for freezing and pop in the freezer until frozen. Enjoy at your leisure!

You can follow the same recipe, substituting the yoghurt for cream to make a delicious alternative to ice cream.

Honeycomb

Making honeycomb is pure magic and if you've got kids, they'll think so too! This sweet treat is so very easy and cheap to make and it's quick too. You will need:

- *4 tbsp golden syrup*
- *200g (7oz) sugar*
- *2 tsp bicarbonate of soda*

Combine the sugar and syrup in a pan over a medium heat and stir until the sugar has dissolved. Bring to the boil and then turn the heat back down, allowing the mixture to simmer for between 5 and 10 minutes making sure the mixture doesn't burn. Remove from the heat and add the bicarbonate of soda. This makes the mixture foam up and so you'll need to work quickly mixing it in before pouring into a greased or lined baking tray. Leave it to set before breaking into pieces. Store in a clean jar or tub.

Fruit Leathers

Making fruit leathers is another good way of using up fruit that is perhaps a little past its best. You can use any fruit you have to hand.

Ingredients

- 4 cups of chopped fruit
- ½ cup of water
- 100g (4oz) sugar
- Juice of ½ lemon

Place the fruit, lemon juice and water in a pan and cook over a medium heat for around 10 minutes. Use a fork or potato masher to break down the cooked fruit and then add the sugar, returning the pan back to the heat.

Stir continuously until the sugar has fully dissolved and allow to simmer for another ten minutes. Use a fork or blender to further break down any lumps so that you have a puree.

Pour the mixture into a lined baking tray so that it is around a quarter of an inch in thickness. Turn the oven to a low setting and place the tin in the centre until the puree has dried out. This could take a few hours. Alternatively you can leave on a worktop but this will take longer. When the fruit leather is dried, cut into strips or chunks and store in an airtight container.

Easy Rocky Road

This is such an easy no bake recipe and requires very little to make. Sweet recipes can sometimes feel frivolous but you what, sometimes we need a little frivolity! Who doesn't want to live deliciously?

Ingredients

- *1 packet of digestive or rich tea biscuits*
- *200g (8oz) of chocolate, whichever you prefer (dark, milk or white)*
- *50 g (2oz) butter*
- *3 tbsp golden syrup*
- *Marshmallows*

Empty your biscuits into a bowl and break them up using the end of a rolling pin so that you have a whole mix of chunks and smaller pieces. Add the marshmallows and set the bowl to one side. In a pan, break the chocolate into small pieces and add the butter and golden syrup. Stir over a low heat until everything is melted together. Pour over the biscuits and marshmallows and mix until everything is completely covered. Turn out into a greased or lined baking tray, pushing the mixture into the corners. Refrigerate for an hour or until the chocolate has set and cut into slices.

If you don't like marshmallows then substitute for dried fruit or other sweets.

Your Own Recipes

Cooking is an adventure, one steeped in learning and experience and so it is only natural that as you make the recipes in this book, you might include your own additions and substitutions. You may have your own favourite recipes you want to include and so use these pages to record any changes to recipes and your own. Happy cooking!

EMMA KATHRYN

Emma Kathryn practises traditional British witchcraft, Vodou and Obeah, a mixture representing her heritage. She lives in the sticks with her family where she reads tarot, practises witchcraft and drink copious amounts of coffee.

ABEAUTIFULRESISTANCE.COM

www.ingramcontent.com/pod-product-compliance
Lightning Source LLC
Chambersburg PA
CBHW072206100526
44589CB00015B/2384